Theos – clear thinking on religion

Theos is the UK's leading religion and society think tank. With our idea: combined circulation of 160 million in the past 10 years, we are shapin about the role of faith in contemporary society by means of high qualit We provide a credible, informed and gracious Christian voice in our ma............. .... conversations.

The Economist calls us "an organisation that demands attention", and Julian Baggini, the influential atheist philosopher, has said "Theos provides rare proof that theology can be interesting and relevant even – perhaps especially – for those who do not believe."

To learn more, check us out on social media:

twitter.com/theosthinktank | facebook.com/theosthinktank | www.theosthinktank.co.uk

Why we exist

Religion has emerged as one of the key public issues of the 21st century, both nationally and globally. Our increasingly religiously-diverse society demands that we grapple with religion as a significant force in public life. Unfortunately, much of the debate about the role and place of religion has been unnecessarily emotive and ill-informed. We exist to change that.

We reject the notion of any possible 'neutral' perspective on these issues. We also reject the idea that religion is a purely private matter or that it is possible to divide public and private values for anyone.

We seek, rather, to recognise and analyse the ethical ideas and commitments that underlie public life and to engage in open and honest public debate, bringing the tradition of Christian social and political thought to bear on current issues. We believe that the mainstream Christian tradition has much to offer for a flourishing society.

What we do

Theos conducts research, publishes reports, and holds debates, seminars and lectures on the intersection of religion, politics and society in the contemporary world. We also provide regular comment for print and broadcast media and briefing and analysis to parliamentarians and policy makers. To date, Theos has produced over 50 research reports focusing on the big issues impacting British society, including welfare (*The Future of Welfare: A Theos Collection*), law (*"Speaking Up" – Defending and Delivering Access to Justice Today*), economics (*Just Money: How Catholic Social Teaching can Redeem Capitalism*), multiculturalism (*Making Multiculturalism Work*) and voting reform (*Counting on Reform*), as well as on a range of other religious, legal, political and social issues.

In addition to our independently-driven work, Theos provides research, analysis and advice to individuals and organisations across the private, public and not-for-profit sectors. Our staff and consultants have strong public affairs experience, an excellent research track record and a high level of theological literacy. We are practised in research, analysis, debate, and media relations.

Where we sit

We are committed to the traditional creeds of the Christian faith and draw on social and political thought from a wide range of theological traditions. We also work with many non-Christian and non-religious individuals and organisations.

Theos was launched with the support of the Archbishop of Canterbury and the Cardinal Archbishop of Westminster, but it is independent of any particular denomination. We are an ecumenical Christian organisation, committed to the belief that religion in general and Christianity in particular has much to offer for the common good of society as a whole. We are not aligned with any point on the party political spectrum, believing that Christian social and political thought cuts across these distinctions.

Join the discussion by becoming a Friend of Theos

Impact how society views Christianity and shape the cultural debate

The Friends' Programme is designed specifically for people who wish to enter the heart of the current debate. When you join, our commitment is to keep you informed, equipped, encouraged and inspired so that you can be a voice in the public square with us.

As a member of the Friends' Programme, you are provided with:

- *Hard copies of all our latest reports* on the most pressing issues – social justice, welfare, politics, spirituality, education, money, atheism, humanism…
- *Free access to our events.* Theos hosts a number of high calibre speakers (e.g. Rowan Williams, Larry Siedentop, Grace Davie) and debates ('Magna Carta and the future of liberty', 'Does humanism need Christianity?'). As a friend, you will receive invitations to all these without charge.
- *A network of like-minded people* who wish to share ideas and collaborate with one another. We host networking events which help you meet fellow Friends and build your own network, allowing ideas to flow and connections to form.
- *Our monthly e-newsletter* which is your one-stop digest for the latest news regarding religion and society.
- **If you join as an Associate**, you are *invited to private functions with the team*, allowing you to discuss upcoming projects, review the latest issues and trends in society, and have your say in where you see the public debate is going.

You can become a Friend or Associate today by visiting our website
www.theosthinktank.co.uk

If you'd prefer additional information, you can write to us directly:
Friends Programme, Theos, 77 Great Peter Street, London, SW1P 2EZ

If you have any inquiries regarding the Programme, you can email us at:
friends@theosthinktank.co.uk

Doing Good Better: The Case for Faith-based Social Innovation

Paul Bickley

Published by Theos in 2017
© Theos

ISBN 978-0-9931969-9-7

Some rights reserved – see copyright licence for details
For further information and subscription details please contact:

Theos
Licence Department
77 Great Peter Street
London
SW1P 2EZ

T 020 7828 7777
E hello@theosthinktank.co.uk
www.theosthinktank.co.uk

contents

acknowledgements

Without wanting to seem grandiose, I would like to thank the many individuals who have encouraged and advised us in this work, especially Francis Davis and Ian Christie at the very outset, and Francis in particular as the source of the 'parable of the ambitious archbishop' with which this report begins.

I am grateful to the many who consented to be interviewed and/or engaged in helpful dialogue about the themes of the report, and those with whom we will engage in the future.

Thanks to my colleagues at Theos who have helped move this research and the report ahead in many ways.

The common characteristic of those mentioned about is that they agree not just that faith groups – from the level of the most modest congregation to international NGOs – contribute hugely to the common good, but also that there is yet untapped potential. I hope this report hints at some of it. As usual, its limitations are my own.

This research has been kindly funded by the Mercer's Company.

executive summary

- Churches and religious institutions are highly motivated to meet social need – they are heavily engaged in social action. The retrenchment of the state in many areas will mean that this increased supply will find increased demand, and vice versa.

- Religious social action needs to find new ways of responding to social problems in systemic, scalable and sustainable ways. Religious groups, organisations and networks need to learn how to "do good better". They should make greater use of the concept, language and practices of "social innovation".

- Social innovation has been defined as a "project or activity that is new, that meets social need, that engages and mobilises beneficiaries, and that to some extent transforms social relations by improving beneficiaries' access to power and resources". Social innovation can help religious organisations evolve and improve. It's not first and foremost about high impact outcomes – which can't always be guaranteed – it's about culture, attitude and processes which could drive greater social impact over the long term.

- In the religious world, there are many factors that influence how social change is done. In this report, we highlight institutions, funding, and attitudes to social entrepreneurship. We think of these in terms of the engine, the fuel, and the driver. These things, taken together, influence the kind of 'journeys' religious organisations tend to make.

Engines – the right institutions for religious social innovation

- There may be ideological and historical barriers to religious institutions thinking about innovation, but these can be overcome by uncovering the religious or theological case for innovation which is present in much religious thought.

- A more significant barrier to innovation is the fact that – with some exceptions – religious social action is delivered through small charities and congregations that have limited capacity for innovation. The place-based nature of religious social action is an important advantage, but this kind of activity needs to be augmented by institutions that will enable and support innovation. Mediating institutions need to put innovation and impact at the heart of their agendas.

- Religious social action should see a greater diversity of social change models as legitimate. There should be more space and support, for instance, for social change through social enterprise or business.

- The wider social innovation world has used innovation 'hubs' to drive innovations through the cycles of conception, experimentation, sustainability and scaling. There are almost none of these in the religious social action sector. There is a strong case for new institutions which explicitly look to support faith-based social innovation.

Fuel – what kinds of funding drive and support innovation?

- Faith-based organisations rely on a range of funding sources – charitable giving, religious grant-making trusts, and some statutory funding. Collectively, these sustain significant amounts of religious social action.

- Some grant-makers prioritise innovation and impact, and some government departments have innovation funds which religious social innovators have been able to access. However, only a limited number of religious charities are engaging with the different kinds of funding sources which tend to power social innovation – this includes social impact investment. Religious social change agents report a struggle to engage with secular grant funders, and feel that they can still be regarded with suspicion.

- Religious social innovation is distinguished from swathes of religious social action by a willingness to engage more seriously with impact measurement and monitoring. Their ability to understand and communicate their impact, and to refine their approach over time, helps them unlock sources of partnership, funding and support.

- Religious institutional investors – who are beginning to experiment in social investment – could drive social innovation by a combined grant making and investment approach which prioritises innovation and impact. Engaging more in social investment relies on church institutional investors identifying investments with an appropriate ratio of risk/return, but their grant-making could fund riskier, experimental approaches to social need.

Drivers – more space for social leadership

- While common endeavour within institutions is vital for religious social innovation, it can't occur without religious social entrepreneurs and innovators – individuals who by insight or experience identify new responses to social needs and pursue them. They are marked out not so much by "heroprenership" as they are by skills in problem definition and insight, creative collaboration, and thought leadership.

- Religious social innovators report feeling marginalised within their own networks – they have to be intrapreneurs before they can be entrepreneurs, championing their cause and approach within their own networks. Clerical leaders are important gatekeepers and decision makers. The success of an innovation depends on capturing their attention and convincing them of the need to redirect their resources.

Conclusions and recommendations

- Religious social innovation depends on getting the right combination of engine, fuel and drivers – new institutions which understand the need for and champion religious social innovation, a greater willingness to monitor and evaluate impact to access different forms of finance and partnership, and greater support for religious social innovators.

introduction

What has been will be again,
what has been done will be done again;
there is nothing new under the sun.

Ecclesiastes 1:9

***

See, I am doing a new thing!
Now it springs up; do you not perceive it?
I am making a way in the wilderness
and streams in the wasteland.

Isaiah 43:19

the parable of the ambitious archbishop

In 2013, in an interview with *Total Politics* magazine, Archbishop Justin Welby relayed a conversation he had had with Errol Damelin, founder and CEO of the payday loan company Wonga: "I've met the head of Wonga and we had a very good conversation and I said to him quite bluntly 'we're not in the business of trying to legislate you out of existence, we're trying to compete you out of existence.' He's a businessman, he took that well."

The comments were well received by others too. Concern had been growing about the increased use of payday loan companies, and campaigners had proposed various legal measures which might prevent their use by vulnerable customers, who could quickly get trapped by the high interest rates, but many had downsides and none were seen as realistic at the time. The intervention was seen as a rare example of the Church of England as a national body using its own resources to meet a widely recognised social need, rather than calling for government action.

The positive story was derailed some days later when it emerged that the Church of England had invested in a venture fund that in turn had invested in Wonga. The revelation brought some embarrassment, but there was a more significant problem with the Archbishop's proposal. He had suggested that credit unions could be at the forefront of the movement to put payday loan companies out of business. While credit unions could provide an important financial service to a limited number of clients, as common bond-based services with strict membership criteria, they were completely unsuited to go up against the instant and online lending of Wonga and its even less socially responsible competitors.

In the years since the Archbishop's comments, the Church of England – alongside many other religious and non-religious organisations – has been active on the affordable finance agenda. It set up a Task Group on Responsible Credit and Savings, chaired by Sir Hector Sants; developed financial education materials for primary schools; and launched the Church Credit Champions Network to work on community finance initiatives through churches.

Wonga's profits have suffered following changes to regulation of the payday loan sector. But it's still in business.

The story is a parable of religious social innovation – promising a "project or activity that is new, that meets social need, that engages and mobilises beneficiaries, and that to some extent transforms social relations by improving beneficiaries' access to power and resources".[1] The Archbishop's stated goal was bold and ambitious but also (given the Church of England's own significant financial reserves, community networks and convening power) achievable. The Church of England can be congratulated for the ways in which it has engaged in the financial inclusion agenda (and which arguably represent social innovations in their own right), but there is no escaping the fact that it did not achieve its goal.

There's a further twist in the story, which we'll come to later.

doing more than ever

It is well known that religious networks and institutions – from the Church of England, through other religious denominations and traditions, to religious charities large and small, international and domestic, and even local congregations – want social change. The signs are that they're doing more than ever.

According to research from New Philanthropy Capital, over one in every four charities in the United Kingdom has a faith basis. These charities have an annual income of around £16 billion, around one quarter of the charity sector's income in England and Wales. Moreover, a higher proportion of faith-based charities (34%) were registered with the Charity Commission in the last ten years than non-faith ones (25%), the figure for Christian charities being 38%.[2]

The National Church and Social Action Survey found that "UK churches have increased the average number of volunteer hours on social action to 114.8m per annum. This is an increase of 16.8% compared with two years earlier and 59.4% compared with four years ago". The survey also suggested that financial investment in social action was increasing, as was the amount of paid staff time dedicated to community activities.[3]

As many as 10 million adults every year could be using church or church-based community services.

Theos' own research with the Church Urban Fund in 2012 identified the sheer reach of faith-based social action. A nationally representative ComRes survey asked interviewees whether they, or an immediate family member, had used church-based community services in the preceding 12 months. Around 1 in 4 respondents had used services provided by churches or church groups. This means that as many as 10 million adults every year could be using church or church-based community services, without even accounting for those provided by non-Christian religious groups.[4]

In view of this mounting evidence, Nick Spencer has argued that religious groups in the UK are seeing a widespread turn to a new 'social liturgy' – "not simply social action that is devoid of any serious theological formation, nor Christian 'worship' that loves God and ignores one's neighbour, but social liturgy – the practice of public commitment to the other that is explicitly rooted in and shaped by love of God".[5]

In recent times, most attention has been directed toward the *amount* of faith-based social action. It focuses on how many projects, how many volunteer hours, how much income for faith-based charities, and so on. These data imply that the reach of faith-based social action (or social liturgy), is rapidly growing.

What is needed is not more but different – new ideas, new approaches, new practices.

We can – and should – celebrate this 'more'. But as the Welby/Wonga incident demonstrates, more is not always what is needed. Sometimes, what is needed is not more but different – new ideas, new approaches, new practices. Many of the great social achievements of religious traditions have not been realised by doing the same thing more, but by pioneering and applying a new approaches.

This raises a range of questions around religious social action which stretch beyond, 'How much are they doing?' What kinds of services and projects do churches and religious organisations tend to offer – why these and not others? How do they emerge and how are they taken up by different congregations or communities? Do they 'work'? How are they funded? Is this or that intervention effective, and how could it be more so? Are there further assets that could be released by faith-based organisations? How are faith-based social activists supported in realising their goals, and how do they work together to achieve their stated objectives or goals? These are not questions about the extent to which faith-based organisations 'do good'. They assume that they do, and then ask, 'How can they do good better?'

Of course, these questions are being asked by faith-based charities and leaders, but not often in a programmatic way. Theos has undertaken this research project in order to at least begin to unpack them. It is part of a strand of work that looks at the activity of faith-based social and charitable action in the UK. It acknowledges that in the 21st century faith will – in secular eyes at least – be more visible in its 'doing good' than in its 'doing God', but argues that the pressure to dis-integrate religious faith and public action can be, is, and should continue to be resisted.

It is often said that faith communities are 'at the forefront' of responding to social need, and in many ways they are. But there is no well-developed conversation in the religious world about the most effective approach to social change.

This conversation is happening in the secular world, framed by the concept of 'social innovation'. This concept – although 'fuzzy' – refers to a set of ideas and practices that have gained significant traction amongst those wanting to achieve social change. In spite of the sheer amount of religious social action, few have sought to make the connection and ask whether any value could be realised in a more structured conversation between the world of religious social action and the world of social innovation.

how not to think about social innovation

One of the reasons that such a structured conversation has not emerged is a lack of a single, comprehensive, yet specific enough definition of what social innovation actually is.

As we suggested above, it has been described as any "project or activity that is new, that meets social need, that engages and mobilises beneficiaries, and that to some extent transforms social relations by improving beneficiaries' access to power and resources". Geoff Mulgan – a key thought leader in the world of social innovation – has described it simply as "new ideas that work to meet unmet needs".[6] Others resort to tighter and more

> *Social innovations are not outcomes that spring from nowhere.*

technical (if less inspiring) definitions – for example, "Acceptable progressive solutions for a whole range of problems of exclusion, alienation, lack of well-being, and also those actions that contribute positively to significant human progress and development".[7] Still other definitions carry heavy ideological baggage – "SI [social innovation] is about social inclusion and about countering or overcoming conservative forces that are eager to strengthen and preserve social exclusion situations".[8]

But beyond these broad terms, scholars agree that "there is no consensus regarding its relevance or specific meaning".[9] Because of this fuzziness in definition, many organisations anchor their accounts in examples.[10] Nesta lists things like first aid, the Open University and code clubs as examples. The Centre for Social Innovation at Stanford Business School offers charter schools, carbon emission tradition, and Fair Trade certification.[11] Used as a post-hoc concept, social innovation is rapidly becoming "an umbrella term for an array of social programs and initiatives deserving attention".[12] In fact TEPSIE – the Theoretical, Empirical and Policy Foundations for Social Innovation in Europe project – has suggested it is still only a "quasi-concept".[13] Too many definitions rely on post-rationalising 'successful' projects as innovation. They then identify this or that trait which 'led to their success' or list shared features.

Given the above, it is hard to imagine what a structured conversation between the world of religious social action and social innovation would look like.

If it's to be useful in the religious space, then, we need to think of social innovation differently. Outcome-based explanations of social innovation – like those set out above – begin with the result. They offer up the large-scale, high impact, projects or institutions – the hospice movement, for instance – as examples of the kind of interventions that we need to see more of. But starting there can be a mistake, encouraging the view that certain innovation just happens – the product of some genius insight or serendipity. Governments, businesses, charities, and funders can begin to idolise innovation services or projects, assuming that they can deliver them effortless impact.[14] Ironically, this can result in less impact – organisations might direct energy and resources to finding the next big idea instead of focusing on refinement, adjustment and creativity within existing projects. This 'social innovation is as social innovation does' approach means that the language and concepts of social innovation are "low in explanatory power and... [offer] little guidance to practitioners."[15]

Instead, we need to use process-based explanations of social innovation. These look at the conception, development, funding scaling and measurement of an innovation. Rather than just the next big idea, social innovation is better understood as "a *process* encompassing the emergence and adoption of *socially creative strategies*, which *reconfigure social relations* in order to actualise a given *social goal*".[16] These emphasise that social innovations are not outcomes that spring from nowhere. Innovators must first work at a small scale, but then may develop and prototype their idea, before looking to see it taken up at scale. Processes like this will require a hospitable environment, and addressing innovation as a process, undergirded by key attitudes and assumptions, will help us to address questions around how innovations take on life (or not) within institutions.

is there such a thing as religious social innovation?

Social innovation doesn't belong to any one sector – though it has its own champions, thought leaders, and think tanks. It happens in the public, private and civic sectors and in ways which muddy the boundary between them.

In *When Bees meet Trees: How large social sector organisations can help to scale social innovation*, Owen Jarvis and Ruth Marvel argue that even many established "social sector organisations are largely disconnected from the world of social innovation and... social innovators who see the potential for partnerships with charities and housing associations often found approaches blocked, ignored or delayed in endless meetings".[17] The question of religious social innovation is the question of how social innovation prospers – or not – with the religious social sector, and why.

It's crucial to say – of course – that doing social innovation is not about superficially adopting a trendy new language to describe what is already there. Rather, it's to ask the kinds of question that the social innovation community is trying to speak to. How do we identify, sustain and scale new responses to all manner of social challenges, and is the religious world a sympathetic context for this kind of approach? Religious social innovation, by the definition above, would relate not just to innovative outcomes, but to the way that social innovation processes are embedded within religious institutions.

The picture is predictably complicated – some religious organisations provide considerable space for innovation, while others might not. Some use the language of innovation, but only in terms of developing more 'culturally relevant' forms of religious community.

What, then, is religious social innovation? What would that more hospitable environment look like? What are the elements of those processes of religious innovation? I would like to propose another metaphor for social religious innovation, which hopefully draws some of the components of religious social innovation into a single image.

We should think of religious social innovation as a vehicle, wherein the three most important parts are the engine – religious institutions, the fuel – whether the right forms of finance for religious social innovation are available, and the driver – the question of leadership and entrepreneurship.

Why select these factors? Are there not significant others we ought to focus on? First, we have already seen that social innovation thinking recognises that innovators can't act alone. Our interviews for this project also attest to the importance of institutions – organisations with influence, resources and power to develop and scale interventions. Second, developments in funding and social finance have been one of the main drivers of social innovation in the UK. Funding for religious social action is one of the main limitations on its growth – we repeatedly encounter evidence which suggests that faith-based providers are regarded with suspicion by a range of funders. Third, it has been suggested that negative attitudes towards social entrepreneurship can limit social innovation, and religious institutions often have strong leadership structures, which may not allow entrepreneurs to emerge.

Other factors that have a significant influence in the emergence of social innovation as a whole – e.g., government policy which encourages innovation – may not have a specific relevance to the religious context.

Our argument is that all of these elements need to operate well, and operate well together. Certain combinations of institutions, funding and leadership will yield certain kinds of religious social action – and the 'wrong' kind of combination may result in social action which is has little – or possibly even a negative – impact.

The question is, what kinds of combination yield social innovation or – more to the point – religious social action with intent and impact?

do we need social innovation?

What's at stake when we talk about social innovation? Why does it matter?

On the one hand, it promises to help churches and faith-based organisations find better ways of achieving their own goals and aspirations when it comes to social change. What approaches might have helped the Church of England establish a Wonga competitor? What prevented it from so doing? What change of culture or organisation would have led to such a goal? As we have said, when it comes to the place for

Social innovation promises to help churches and faith-based organisations find better ways of achieving their own goals and aspirations.

faith in the 21st century Britain, faith-based organisations will often be judged on their capacity to achieve social change.

But there are other, more fundamental, reasons than religious traditions somehow proving their worth. In one of the only extended reflections on the relationship between social innovation and the Christian faith, L Gregory Jones sets out the case:

> Most people are hungry for innovation. We are hungry for new ways of living and doing things that can chart better paths forward. We are hungry for innovation because we know that we are facing challenges that are "complex," problems that are "wicked." These words convey that our challenges and problems intersect in ways that make them more difficult to address than just being "complicated" or "hard." Indeed, our challenges and problems intersect so deeply that we need multiple strategies because no single approach can "solve" the challenge or "fix" the problem… We have a looming sense that too much of our world is in a state of degeneration or disruption, that older institutions and patterns of life are decaying and dying. We have a sense that we need something new.[18]

Jones is not merely referring here to religious institutions, but making a broader case about the need to adapt to social, political and economic change.

It is no coincidence that there has been rapid growth in the social innovation industry since 2008. Although the processes of decay began before, we have in the last decade become acutely aware that old 'social technologies' are in a state of disrepair. As Angela Merkel has said, "Europe today accounts for just over 7 per cent of the world's population, produces around 25 per cent of global GDP and has to finance 50 per cent of global social spending".[19] In many public institutions, there is a sense that we are achieving a point of maximum 'efficiency' – that there is no more juice that can be squeezed.

One doesn't need to believe that we are on the road to 'minarchism' (a night-watchman state) to recognise that the state – particularly at the municipal level – is unlikely to substantially increase levels of public provision. The most likely future is one where the state is a substantial provider of islands of public services, but increasingly looks to other parties – not necessarily corporates, but social enterprises, and community organisations (we should all hope) – to provide them. Other means of funding have been and will continue to be identified (e.g., social impact bonds), and new forms of public service will emerge.

Religious organisations will be part of this much diversified and more complex space, no doubt particularly serving those who fall off the edge of public provision. The question is what role they will play, and that will be determined in substantial part by their ability to adjust to new challenges and scale their social endeavours.

research methodology and report structure

The objective of this research project is to understand how innovation processes operate – where they do – in religious institutions, and set out how faith communities can benefit from engaging with social innovation thinking and practices (and vice-versa).

In preparation for this report we have looked at the ever-broadening literature on social innovation. We wanted to understand various accounts and definitions of social innovation, ask what drives secular social innovation efforts, and then establish its relevance to the faith-based social action agenda.

We then interviewed a range of social innovators – though virtually none would call themselves such – in order to garner their perspective on what it is to be a social innovator in a religious context. These 'innovators' were active in the faith-based social change and social action space, either as institutional leaders or simply social entrepreneurs. The majority of interviewees were Christian, but we also spoke to organisations and entrepreneurs in other religious traditions.

Our thesis was that, while there is a significant amount of religious social action, there is limited formal engagement with the social innovation agenda. We wanted to understand why, whether this could change, and what could be gained if it did. It is crucial to note that there is a good religious innovation story to be told, though it is fair to say that it is not one that is particularly well connected to or recognised by the rest of the social innovation world.

In the first chapter, we will explore the institutional context of and for religious social innovation. Are religious communities receptive to social innovation, and if not – why not? We will consider some of the strengths and weaknesses of the religious context as a space for innovation, and argue that although innovation may look different, it is vitally important.

In the second chapter we will consider the crucial question of how religious social innovation can be resourced. If religious social innovations are to achieve greater scale, then sustainability will be a key factor. We will argue that religious social innovation is detached from the social investment world. We ask why that might be, and propose solutions.

In the third chapter, we will consider the place of the religious social innovator in the context of wider views of leadership within religious institutions. Although social innovation is not just a matter of individual genius or creativity, social innovation does require individual talent, creativity and resilience. We will consider how religious institutions support not just innovations but innovators.

Our analysis, put simply, is that sometimes one of these elements is missing or misfiring – religious social innovation therefore doesn't have the horsepower that it might in other circumstances. Doing good better means tuning the engine – making sure we have the right kind of institutions; making sure they have enough fuel – ensuring that there is sufficient finance; and ensuring that we have the right kind of environment for drivers. This is not meant to sound unduly pessimistic – the religious world has engines, access to fuel and very many drivers. The objective is to understand how they are operating together – or not – and how to ensure their best functioning.

Between each chapter we will turn to a fleshed-out and extended case study in order to reflect practically on ways in which innovation has taken place. These are not intended to be representative of the data a whole, but to root the analysis in real world examples. To labour our metaphor, these are occasions when we know that engine, fuel and driver have come together, even if not in complete harmony. A brief look at their journeys should help us understand something of what needs to happen in order to see more religious social innovation.

The report concludes with a realistic assessment of the usefulness of social innovation thinking for religious social action. We will make recommendations for how faith-based agencies and institutions can foster innovation or, put more simply, how they can do good better.

introduction – reference

1   TEPSIE, 'Doing Social Innovation: A Guide for Practitioners'. A deliverable of the project: "The theoretical, empirical and policy foundations for building social innovation in Europe" (TEPSIE), European Commission – 7th Framework Programme, Brussels: European Commission, DG Research, p. 9. http://www.tepsie.eu/images/documents/research_report_final_web.pdf (accessed 18 April 2017).

2   Rachel Wharton and Lucy de Las Casas, *What a Difference a Faith Makes: Insights on Faith-Based Charities* (New Philanthropy Capital, 2017). Available at http://www.thinknpc.org/publications/what-a-difference-faith-makes/ (accessed 19 April 2017).

3   Geoff Knott, *Investing More for the Common Good: National Church and Social Action Survey Results* (Jubilee+, 2014). Available at https://jubilee-plus.org/docs/Report-National-Church-Social-Action-Survey-2014-Executive-Summary.pdf (accessed 19 April 2017).

4   Paul Bickley, *Good Neighbours: How Churches Help Communities Flourish* (Theos, 2014); http://www.theosthinktank.co.uk/publications/2014/07/10/good-neighbours-how-churches-helpcommunities-flourish

5   Nick Spencer, *Doing Good: A Future for Christianity in the 21st Century* (Theos, 2016), p. 49-50.

6   Geoff Mulgan, *Social Innovation: What It Is, Why It Matters, and How It Can Be Accelerated* (The Young Foundation, 2007), Available at http://eureka.sbs.ox.ac.uk/761/1/Social_Innovation.pdf (accessed 19 April 2017).

7   Frank Moulaert, Diana MacCallum, Abid Mehmood, *The International Handbook on Social Innovation: Collective Action, Social Learning and Transdisciplinary Research* (Edward Elgar, 2013), p. 16.

8   Moulaert et al., *Handbook*, p. 16.

9   Kristen Pue, Christian Vandergeest, Dan Breznitz, *Toward a Theory of Social Innovation* (University of Toronto, 2016). Available at http://munkschool.utoronto.ca/ipl/files/2016/02/SOCINN.White_.Paper_.pdf

10   Nesta, 'Everyday Social Innovations', http://www.nesta.org.uk/news/everyday-social-innovations

11   Stanford Business, 'Defining Social Innovation', https://www.gsb.stanford.edu/faculty-research/centers-initiatives/csi/defining-social-innovation

12   Pue et al. *Theory*, p. 2.

13   TEPSIE, 'Social Innovation Theory and Research: A Summary of the Findings from TEPSIE.' A deliverable of the project: "The theoretical, empirical and policy foundations for building social innovation in Europe" (TEPSIE), European Commission – 7th Framework Programme, Brussels: European Commission, DG Research, p. 10. Available at https://iupe.files.wordpress.com/2015/11/tepsie-research_report_final_web.pdf (accessed 27 April 2017).

14   Christian Seelos and Johanna Mair, 'Innovation Is Not the Holy Grail', *Stanford Social Innovation Review*, (Fall 2012) https://ssir.org/articles/entry/innovation_is_not_the_holy_grail

15 Ibid.

16 Pue et al. *Theory*, p. 10.

17 Owen Jarvis and Ruth Marvel, '"When Bees Meet Trees": Scaling Social Innovation Through Existing Organisations', RSA, 15 October 2013. Available at https://www.thersa.org/discover/publications-and-articles/rsa-blogs/2013/10/when-bees-meet-trees-scaling-social-innovation-through-existing-organisations---guest-post (accessed 27 April 2017).

18 L. Gregory Jones, *Christian Social Innovation: Renewing Wesleyan Witness* (Abingdon Press, 2016) Kindle Location 90-91.

19 Quentin Peel, 'Merkel Warns on Cost of Welfare', *Financial Times*, 16 December 2012. Available at https://www.ft.com/content/8cc0f584-45fa-11e2-b7ba-00144feabdc0 (accessed 19 April 2017).

case study – Million Minutes' Courtyard Project

Million Minutes is a Catholic charity which – according to CEO Danny Curtin – exists to leverage people and resources into meaningful social change, with a particular focus on enabling young people. "We do this through what we call leadership, by which we mean leading active lives. We equip people to lead an active life, which is basically to put the principles of Catholic Social Teaching into practice, wherever they are".

Originally a grant-making organisation, Million Minutes has begun to pilot a new Catholic Youthwork project called The Courtyard. Curtin told us how he was prompted to initiate the project by listening to Susanne Rauprich of the National Council of Voluntary Youth Services speak on the subject of knife crime:

> She was virtually crying, and told this faith-based audience that they have people and plant [buildings and facilities] and resources in virtually every community in the country, and that they had a real potential to save lives.

The project is built around resources that aspire to help young people tell their story, and so rediscover their God-given meaning and purpose. It begins with detached youthwork, but then offers young people community space within the church if they want it. Curtin is concerned that churches are comfortable doing 'youth ministry' for Catholic young people, but no longer have the resources or models to work with others. On the other side of the equation, fewer and fewer local authorities are investing in youthwork.

In designing the project, Million Minutes has drawn on the best methodologies in volunteer engagement and youthwork practice, but re-developed them to be delivered in a Catholic context. With the project largely delivered by volunteers, some of the models – particularly the monitoring – have had to be simplified. Curtin is clear that the vision is to see 2000 Catholic churches re-engaged with youthwork across communities, unpacking latent talents and resources that aren't always well engaged by church focused activities.

what's the social innovation?

As with so much social innovation, the Courtyard project is at least as much recovery as it is invention. Curtin looks back to a time when the vast majority of youth work was delivered by churches and other religious organisations. There is an 'intrapreneurial' process here, which is about unlocking the skills and agency of Catholic volunteers in exciting new ways. There is also considerable borrowing, with Million Minutes taking approaches piloted elsewhere and making them work in a different context and in a different language – that of Catholic social teaching.

Danny Curtin also reflects on his own journey as an 'innovator':

> Why do I end up doing this stuff – why do people see me as a social entrepreneur? It's just because people invested in me. I thought that they were supporting what I was doing, but they were supporting me as well. That's what we want for other young people.

engine: religious institutions

In the introduction we set out how social innovation shouldn't be understood primarily as an outcome alone, but rather as a process embedded within institutions and underpinned by a set of attitudes and assumptions.

We will explore religious social innovation from three angles, or as three components of a system. The first, set out below, is what we call the 'engine' – that is the institutional context in which religious social action takes place. Is it hospitable to new approaches – to religious social innovation?

the national picture

In a 2016 paper, the Economist Intelligence Unit set out a social innovation index, intended to show which countries were providing the best conditions for social innovation.[1] The index was built around four pillars, with the 'policy and institutional framework' pillar being weighted most strongly (the others were financing, social entrepreneurship and civil society). Countries were given a score on each pillar, determined by how they performed across a range of indicators.

The indicators for the policy and institutional framework pillar were a) the existence of national policy for social innovation; b) social innovation research and impact; c) a legal framework for social enterprises; d) effectiveness of system in policy implementation; and e) the rule of law. The United Kingdom was rated first in the world for its policy and institutional framework pillar, contributing to its overall second place in the whole index. The UK has a national policy for social innovation and has actively supported it with measures under the Big Society umbrella. It also has dedicated legal forms for social enterprises (for example, Community Interest Companies), and the right kind of financial institution (e.g., Big Society Capital and financial intermediaries) to channel appropriate forms of capital towards charities and social enterprises.

It's also worth noting that the United Kingdom also has an ecology of social innovation organisations and academic centres that are given over to understanding, promoting and resourcing social innovation (e.g., Nesta, the Young Foundation, the Skoll Foundation, The Social Innovation Partnership). These institutions represent a very strong background culture of social innovation.

minding the gap

Even if the United Kingdom is one of the best places in the world for social innovation, religion is still surprisingly absent from the social innovation world.

Even if the United Kingdom is one of the best places in the world for social innovation, religion is still surprisingly absent from the social innovation world.

Is it that social innovation doesn't do God, or that doing God means you don't do innovation? We suspect the latter, in the sense that there are some religious individuals who have a high profile in the social innovation world, but religious institutions are rarely engaged. In other words, it is not that religious institutions struggle to get a seat at the table but that, with honourable exceptions (such as the Cathedral Innovation Centre in Portsmouth), there seems to be little appetite for engagement in the social innovation conversation.

Why? It is paradoxical. Religion in general and Christianity in particular at one time was a profound 'innovation' – a disruption and development of existing religious traditions. It grew through innovation – specifically caring for the poor of the Roman world. It innovates to the present day at both small and large scale in the UK, and internationally at greater scale. But it rarely engages formally with the social innovation world. Is this indicative of a lack of appetite for greater intentionality in social change – the process of learning to do good, better?

Before addressing the question of the how the religious institutional context allows for religious social innovation, it's worth exploring some of the barriers of culture and language.

religion at the centre, religion at the margin

Historically, to call something an innovation was far more likely to be a criticism than a complement. Puritans used the word to assail those they considered to be distorting the doctrine and the discipline of the church. They in turn were assailed with it by those who claimed that they were subverting the authority of the church by failing to submit to the bishops. In politics, republicans and socialists were slurred with accusations of innovation.[2]

What turned innovation from a swear word to a purr word? Nothing less than modernity itself, with its implicit commitment to human material progress. Political and industrial revolutions demonstrated that there was such a thing as 'creative destruction' long before Joseph Schumpeter got round to coining the phrase. For all the trauma of tearing down the old order, what replaced it could be better. Some argue that social innovation in its current incarnation began to get traction in the radical student protests of the 1960s.[3]

It may be that ambivalence towards innovation can be partly explained by the position of dominant religious traditions as buttresses of the prevailing social order. Religion belongs with 'tradition', 'heritage', and 'orthodoxy'. When religion is a foundation of order, and nestles comfortably at the heart of society and culture, what does it have to gain from reformation, revolution, or innovation?

Where religious social innovation has emerged, it has often been from the religious margins – the Salvation Army, pushing against the religious and social establishment of the day; the Quakers, excluded from the core of religious and social life; or the Catalan Catholicism of Father José María Arizmendiarrieta, founder of the Mondragón cooperative movement. This isn't to say that religious social innovation necessarily goes with liturgical or theological innovation. Radical social thinking can emerge from orthodox theology – indeed, religious social innovation won't necessarily be the rejection of a theological tradition but a return to the root of it. But social innovation is more likely to occur in religious traditions that are not comfortably part of the establishment, and in those which are forced to adopt a 'missionary position'.

> Social innovation is more likely to occur in religious traditions that are not comfortably part of the establishment.

metaphor matters

It's important to notice that social innovation language is metaphorical. The assumption that technological development is the process that carries humanity ahead is very powerful, and the phrase 'social innovation' takes these processes of technological development, which in turn drive changes in economic and social life, and applies them to human community and relationships.

Once 'innovation' had sprung to life, not as a mere noun attached to concrete material processes but as a system of thought and practice, it seems there was hardly any area of life to which it could not be applied. Any process that could be thought of as a machine-like system, functioning according to a set of rules that can be adjusted, tuned-up, re-thought or replaced, would be open to innovation.

At the turn of the 20th and 21st centuries, two American sociologists – William Fielding Ogburn and Arland D Weeks – argued that the arena of 'social invention' ("invention that is not mechanical and that is not a discovery in the natural science") needed to be recognised and pursued.[4] Their lists of 'social inventions' bear a striking – while not exact – resemblance to what, in the last 10-15 years, have been identified as social innovation. Ogburn listed day nurseries, basketball, group insurance, legal aid societies, minimum wage law, and the Ku Klux Klan (!), amongst many others. Weeks' list was more general – the League of Nations, medicine, idle time, and 'moral code' – but the point was the same. These were things that human beings had 'invented' in order to help them live better lives, just as hotter furnaces had been developed to make better iron. "Just as there has been a field for mechanical invention, so is there a field for social invention?" asked Weeks. His answer was yes, but "social invention is miles behind mechanical... The possibilities of social invention are as great as were the mechanical possibilities that lay before the early inventors of machines".[5]

Peter Drucker deployed the language of innovation to individual organisations. Innovation for him was the

> specific function of entrepreneurship, whether in an existing business, a public service institution, or a new venture started by a lone individual in the family... [which] creates new wealth-producing resources or endows existing resources with enhanced potential for creating wealth.[6]

The simple and powerful analogy is between a new technology generating greater profit, and new business practices which would likewise create value.

The change of language is the same thing as the change of posture and a change of thinking, and this has implications for how religious organisations engage in social innovation. Religious networks don't think in technological metaphors, but agrarian, biological, civic and relational ones: vines, bodies, cities and families.

One effect of this is that religious charities can be resistant to the idea of measuring social impact. That's not mere laziness, but a sense of their work as an 'ecology' rather than a system. Vines bear fruit, bodies display health, cities are at peace, members of families love one another.

Religious charities can be resistant to the idea of measuring social impact.

None of these ways of thinking move very easily in the social innovation space, which trades in social value, impact and outcomes.

It's not for this essay to suggest that religious institutions need to change their thinking and self-perception in order that they might be more socially innovative – in any case, such changes would likely be superficial, even embarrassing. The point is that these influence how religious institutions relate to and learn from other worlds than their own. In 2014, there was something of a furore in the Church of England when Lord Green of Hurstpierpoint prepared a report for the Church of England on 'Talent Management for Future Leaders and Leadership Development for Bishops and Deans', which advocated MBA – style training amongst a talent pool of senior leaders. The theologian and Dean of Christ Church, Martyn Percy, suggested that the report "has no point of origination in theological or spiritual wisdom. Instead, on offer is a dish of basic contemporary approaches to executive management, with a little theological garnish."[7]

It is unlikely that the way to see a greater engagement with the language and practices of social innovation amongst religious institutions is to go 'over the head' of core theological commitments. That said, if religious social action is to move toward religious social innovation, it will need to learn to talk – and even sometimes to think – differently. There are theological traditions which could underpin greater engagement with social innovation, but the most obvious starting point might be one of humility. Religious groups can be guilty of over-claiming, or assuming that 'we know how to do social action', or that the other social change agents need to learn our language. On the contrary, sometimes we need to learn theirs, and yet continue to communicate and act in distinctive ways.

institutional diversity

If we are to see religious social innovation emerge to a greater degree, then innovation thinking will need to be embedded in existing religious institutions. As with the wider social innovation world, there may also be a need for new institutions to support religious social innovation.

Of course, there is already an incredible diversity of institutions in the religious world. Even single religious denominations can be significantly more complex than large social sector organisations. Rev Philip Krinks, Director of the St Martin's Partnership, told us:

> The thing about the Church of England is, it's really a family of institutions – the Church Army, the Church Urban Fund... the work of the Bishops in the Lords, diocesan social action groups, major parishes with huge programmes of their own... the truth is, it's an institution of institutions.

Congregational level activity can only manage so much of the social innovation process.

However, in spite of significant institutional diversity, there is a paucity of the kind of institutions that could engage in questions around innovation in the religious world.

Much mission and social action in the religious world takes place at the congregational level. This is considered to be one of the main strengths of religious social action – it means that 'services' have a face. At best they are highly relational and responsive to varying need. Arguably, this kind of relatively small scale activity gives the opportunity of social entrepreneurs to experiment and trial new responses or interventions.

But congregational level activity can only manage so much of the social innovation process. A parish or a congregation experiences constraints on resources that will limit it to ameliorative action – by its very nature, scaling a project will require partnerships that span the fairly narrow geographical boundaries of single congregations, and it can't be assumed that the next parish along – independently led – will adopt the same approach. The social innovation conversation is best had at a middle layer, which can focus both on practical delivery and strategic issues around the 'how' of social change.

There are examples of such meso-level organisations emerging. Community franchising (e.g., Cinnamon Network) is one. The Church Urban Fund 'Together' Joint Ventures are another. Parachurch organisations can achieve scale – especially successfully in the case of the Trussell Trust. They achieve scale by replication, but don't always have innovation at the heart of their approach. Indeed, avowedly they tend to replicate congregation-based social interventions.

Non-Christian religious communities have established new institutions to embed social innovation in their community. We spoke to Shoshana Boyd Gelfand at JHub, a community which supports positive social change in the British Jewish Community and beyond. She spoke about how the Jewish community had a strong tradition of social care for those within the Jewish community, but there was a critique that this was too much their focus. Before JHub was established, they carried out a mapping exercise, and found that there were a number of Jewish organisations working for wider social change. JHub was launched to support, help 'incubate' and develop those organisations. Many of the services it provides are not in themselves innovative – for instance, they source pro bono legal advice on which legal form (e.g., charity, social enterprise, Community Interest Company) an initiative should take – but it provides the institutional context in which innovation can take place.

> *The relative absence of this kind of institution implies an overall lack of intent.*

It is striking that JHub is a lonely example of a faith-based social innovation hub. Of course, some of the services offered by JHub may be provided informally and in other ways, but the relative absence of this kind of institution implies an overall lack of intent, and an assumption that innovative solutions will find a way through without formalised support.

bridging the gap

There is a gap between the worlds of religious social action and social innovation. That gap emerges from the overly comfortable religious 'establishment', differences in language, and a lack of the kind of institutions that occupy the middle space between micro-level social action and macro-level political engagement.

Are there ways of bridging the gap, of turning religious social action into religious social innovation?

We have already hinted at them above. While religious networks are rooted in traditions of thought, this doesn't mean that religion is wholly sterile or that they're disinterested in change. They are deeply marked by the tension between the way the world is and the way the world could or should be. This is the instinct that has led them to 'invent' again and again – the monastic tradition, schools, hospices and hospitals, early forms of probation, arguably the idea of charity itself.

social innovation and Christian social thought

Many religious traditions have bodies of theological reflection that describe and underpin religious social action. Catholic Social Teaching is probably the best developed and sustained of these. What defines the particular teachings that together make up CST is a matter of debate, but they certainly include the preferential option for the poor, solidarity and subsidiarity. CST is further defined with every new papal encyclical or 'apostolic exhortation', and has recently covered new ground in engaging with the 2008 financial crash and with environmental issues.

CST clearly offers grounding for the Catholic community to do good, but it also creates space for innovation. Some of the core themes of CST directly lend themselves to it. In his Theos report on Catholic Social Teaching and Catholic Charities, Ben Ryan observes:

> Subsidiarity functions for CST essentially as a corrective to twentieth century political discourses. Against socialism it puts forward the idea that real justice is found in letting people and organisations take action for themselves where they are able to, thereby valuing non-state and local agency over the state. Against some models of capitalism, it also suggests that there is a place for different levels in society to take action; people are not simply isolated and expected to stand only on their own two feet.[8]

What is interesting here is that CST is not only about the *what* – care for the poor, or regard for creation. It is also about the *how* – the means of achieving social goods. Subsidiarity as a broad principle takes the view that agency should reside at the lowest level possible. In other words, civil society should act to care for the vulnerable where possible, and the state should act where necessary. Social innovation is a way that changed view of agency can be put into practice.

Pope Francis' apostolic exhortation *Evangelii Gaudium* is particularly useful for creating a theological space for the idea of social innovation. The exhortation celebrates the possibility of 'newness' in the Church's mission.

> As Saint Irenaeus writes: "By his coming, Christ brought with him all newness". With this newness he is always able to renew our lives and our communities, and even if the Christian message has known periods of darkness and ecclesial weakness, it will never grow old. Jesus can also break through the dull categories with which we would enclose him and he constantly amazes us by his divine creativity. Whenever we make the effort to return to the source and to recover the original freshness of the Gospel, new avenues arise, new paths of creativity open up, with different forms of expression, more eloquent signs and words with new meaning for today's world. Every form of authentic evangelization is always "new".[9]

He goes on to ask his readers

> to abandon the complacent attitude that says: "We have always done it this way". I invite everyone to be bold and creative in this task of rethinking the goals, structures, style and methods of evangelization in their respective communities. A proposal of goals without an adequate communal search for the means of achieving them will inevitably prove illusory.[10]

Although the distinction between means and ends is often unhelpful, here it allows for significant latitude in the ways the Catholic community might act to achieve its mission (evangelisation, in Catholic Social Teaching, has a strong social and public as well as personal dimension). In other words, there is a direct invitation not to preserve traditions in aspic, but to use whatever means might be at our disposal to achieve goals.

This is not a merely Catholic sentiment. Jonny Baker, who oversees a Church Mission Society course on Pioneer Mission, spoke to us about the breadth and importance of a sense of mission and a need for imagination.

> *The start point is about imagination.*

> For us the start point is about imagination... In the world of missiology, God is involved in the transformation of all things and our mission is to join in with that... It includes the personal, societal and political. The Church is missionary by

nature, but the Church forgets that – one of the problems around innovation is that the Church asks how it can do church better rather than thinking about the transformation of the community that it's in.

Social innovation may be best understood less as an ideology than as a form of practical wisdom, of 'phronesis'. Theologian Kevin Vanhoozer describes this as "a form of virtuous perception and disciplined improvisation that leads to creative understanding" and "an ensemble of character traits that… come to expression in acts aimed at achieving the good".[11] In short, religious institutions have strong narratives around why they should seek social change or social transformation, but they focus less on cultivating the skills – or indeed the virtues – which could help them do so more effectively. Social innovation could be understood as one frame for this "how to" kind of knowledge.

tuning the institutional engine

Finally, then, what kind of practical adjustments could be made to make the institutional context more hospitable for religious social innovation?

First, the values and attitudes of social innovation should be adopted in existing institutions. At this level, it doesn't really matter what an organisation exists to do. Some might focus on grassroots campaigning, others on elite level political engagement. The question of social innovation is one of ambition and organisation – do these institutions organise themselves for maximum impact? Tim Thorlby, from the Contextual Theology Centre, suggested that religious social action focuses too much on mercy and charity, and not enough on questions around justice and the economic flourishing. At the heart of social innovation there is a desire not just to respond to social need, but to act in ways which disrupt and change systems and markets.

> At the heart of social innovation there is a desire not just to respond to social need, but to act in ways which disrupt and change systems.

Religious communities – and entrepreneurs – may have to overcome internal hurdles if they want to get religious networks to think about system change. Duncan Milwain, a Christian lawyer closely involved with setting up the Real Junk Food project, a secular charity tackling food waste through food interception, said that it was easier to convince Christians of the need to tackle food poverty than it was to convince them of the need for system change in the food economy. The point is not that practical action should be accompanied with political campaigning, but that practical action can and should be transformative rather than ameliorative.

Larger religious charities could follow where secular organisations have led, recruiting people responsible for managing and engaging with social innovation. Many have 'theological advisers'; why not innovation advisers, who can champion the approach, and actively look for innovations from elsewhere? Their purpose would not be to produce innovations, but to embed innovation as a process.

Second, religious social action should see a greater diversity of social change models as legitimate. The stock model of religious social action is a small local charity or, increasingly, 'community franchising', where tried and tested projects are adopted, off the rack, by local congregations at a relatively modest scale. Community franchising is arguably an innovation in its own right – particularly in the sense of scaling through replication in the religious context, but all the projects are roughly of the same kind. There is little space, for instance, for social change through social enterprise.

This might seem to write off or denigrate the considerable efforts of thousands of religious volunteers across the country who give time and resources to ensure that people are fed, clothed and befriended. It is not, but it is to ask the age-old question of how to save people from drowning by stopping them falling into the river, rather than by fishing them out downstream. Again, not all social innovation is 'disruptive' – much of it might come into the 'sustained' category of innovation – a long term commitment to expand and improve existing models, rather than create ex nihilo. Foodbanks, for example, have spread across the UK in a remarkable way – but Alison Inglis-Jones from the Trussell Trust described to us how they're evolving beyond the simple provision of emergency food support, working at a local and national level to help people better negotiate the benefit system. Even interventions which begin with meeting basic material needs can be open to innovation.

Third, there is a need for dedicated hubs or social innovation communities. These will supplement the ongoing work of faith-based charities, congregations and religious denominations but their task would not be to develop more of the same, but to support faith-based entrepreneurs through the whole innovation process.

chapter 1 – references

1   Naka Kondo, 'Old problems, new solutions: Measuring the capacity for social innovation across the world', The Economist Intelligence Unit, (2016). Available at https://www.eiuperspectives. economist.com/technology-innovation/old-problems-new-solutions-measuring-capacity-social-innovation-across-world-0/white-paper/old-problems-new-solutions-measuring-capacity-social-innovation-across-world (accessed 27 April 2017).

2   Emma Green, 'Innovation: The History of a Buzzword', The Atlantic, 20 June 2017. Available at https://www.theatlantic.com/business/archive/2013/06/innovation-the-history-of-a-buzzword/277067/

3   Moulaert et al., Handbook (op. cit.), p. 16

4   Benoît Godin, 'Innovation: The History of a Category' (2008). Available at http://www.csiic.ca/PDF/IntellectualNo1.pdf, p. 30

5   Quoted in Godin, p. 31

6   Peter Drucker, 'The Discipline of Innovation', Harvard Business Review, August 2002. Available at https://hbr.org/2002/08/the-discipline-of-innovation

7   Paul Handley, 'Plan to groom "talent" for high office in C of E', Church Times, 12 December 2014. Available at https://www.churchtimes.co.uk/articles/2014/12-december/news/uk/plan-to-groom-talent-for-high-office-in-c-of-e

8   Ben Ryan, Catholic Social Thought and Catholic Charities in Britain Today: Need and Opportunity. (Theos, 2016), p. 35.

9   Apostolic Exhortation, Evangelii Gaudium. (2013), p 11. Available at http://w2.vatican.va/content/dam/francesco/pdf/apost_exhortations/documents/papa-francesco_esortazione-ap_20131124_evangelii-gaudium_en.pdf (accessed 27 April 2017).

10   Evangelli Gaudium, p. 30.

11   Kevin Vanhoozer, The Drama of Doctrine: A Canonical-linguistic Approach to Christian Theology. (Westminster: John Knox Press, 2005), p. 332

case study – family support services

During the course of this research we came across three organisations that – quite separately – had come up with the same solution for supporting families in need.

Fegans is a 147 year old charity and former provider of children's homes. Now, it offers counselling for children and young people and parenting support. The majority of their work is carried on a contractual basis with schools and local authorities, though they also offer counselling in their own children's centres – often providing pro bono support to families who can't afford fees. They have started partnering with local churches to train volunteers to provide specialist and high-end parenting support.

Comparatively speaking, Safe Families for Children is a young organisation. Set up in 2013, it uses volunteers to provide three types of support to families; Host Families who offer respite care in their home for children for a couple of nights to a couple of weeks; Family Friends offering befriending and mentoring support and Resource Friends who of goods and services to resource stretched families. This is early intervention support to families at to reduce the number of children ending up in care. Again, the vast majority of their volunteers are drawn from churches.

Vennture Family Pastors, a re-incarnation of what was the Hereford City Mission, run a 'family pastors' programme. Family Pastors are trained volunteers – again, often based in churches – who can work with the family to help them "gain the support they need to make changes, find solutions to their challenges and bring new hope into their lives". These volunteers work with the family for one hour a week for a period of six to nine months, focusing on key targets and outcomes.

Each of these projects takes maximum advantage of one of the core strengths of church-based social action – a large reserve of volunteers that, with appropriate training, can significantly reduce the burden on public services. Ian Soars – Director of children and family counselling charity Fegans – quoted in NSPCC statistic that suggested that two million children in the UK were in need of intervention from social services and said: "Whichever way you look at it, the church has to be part of the answer".

These organisations all work closely with statutory services, and thus become guarantors for that significant reservoir of volunteers, ensuring that they are appropriately vetted and trained. Not that accessing or managing those volunteers is easy – all the organisations reported having to work hard to encourage churches with an inward focus to support their work, and indeed to ensure that volunteers acted appropriately in the context in which they were volunteering. Robert Thomas of Vennture stated that they sometimes have to select against "people on a mission – who think that they have the answers". Positively, these agencies acted as intermediaries, interpreting between the different language and culture of statutory services and religious groups in order to realise the opportunities for collaboration.

what's the social innovation?

These groups were operating at a real point of tension, where statutory services are stretched to their limit and in need of "before the event" interventions, as Robert Thomas called them. Working in the statutory sector forced them to measure outcomes and impacts effectively. With the help of a Department of Education innovation grant, Safe Families for Children is scaling rapidly, and is now operating in seven different locations across the United Kingdom. All of them, however, reported feeling that they were 'on the back foot', obliged to provide extra assurances about the quality of their services in order to overcome suspicions about explicitly religious organisations.

fuel: innovation funding

In chapter 1 we looked at the engine of social innovation – that is, the institutional framework in which social innovators act. We turn now to the question of funding, or what we call the 'fuel' of religious social innovation.

Social innovation needs sustainable funding. Indeed, if a social innovation is not financially sustainable, then it can barely qualify as such. As the Economist Intelligence Unit notes, the options for funding are broad. Part of the appeal of social innovation is the possibility of taking advantage of non-charitable sources of finance.

Again, the United Kingdom has created a supportive environment for social innovation. The space includes multiple funding options beyond charitable sources. How religious social innovation fares in this funding world is an important factor in both its flourishing and of its ability to command attention from the wider social innovation world.

whose (funding) round is it?

There are four key sources for social innovation funding in the UK.

First, there is a commercial element. It is one of the marks of social innovation that it is far less restrictive about what form an organisation has to take in order to have a social purpose. Therefore some social innovations may fund themselves entirely through commercial activity. Managed to repeat an entire sentence. One of the main legal vehicles for social innovative projects – Community Interest Companies (CICs) – are permitted to have a social purpose and make a profit which can then be paid to trustees. Charities, of course, are also permitted to trade and make profit, but if they do the profits belong to the charity.

> *Some social innovations may fund themselves entirely through commercial activity.*

Second, there are charitable funds. Much innovation occurs in the charitable world, and is funded in exactly the same way as other activities for public benefit. Even if a social innovation or social enterprise has a commercial viability, grant making trusts have a role.

No investor, even an impact investor, will simply hand over capital to an undeveloped idea that has not been piloted or evaluated. Like any potential investor, they need information. So grant funders often have a role in kick-starting innovation, and some focus specifically on innovation. Again, many charities may be quietly and steadily innovating within the context of 'services' they already deliver.

Third, some innovation depends directly on public investments of one kind or another. Some countries have publicly funded innovation hubs. In the UK, a number of government departments (e.g., the Department for Education, the Department for International Development) have innovation funds which seek to catalyse, support and scale solutions to particular policy goals. Occasionally, governments may simply grant funds to ideas which they think are worth supporting.

Fourth, we have the growing arena of social and impact investment. This agenda is about making sure that social enterprises, charities, or innovators, can get access to loan or investment capital where that is appropriate to their business. Financing in this way can create a shorter route to scale social innovation and provide an opportunity for investors to look for social as well as financial return. It's seen as a more sustainable way of ensuring investment than traditional public sector contracting and grant-making, and allows innovations to act in ways that grants or charitable support would not. The 2010-15 Coalition government put considerable effort in here, creating Big Society Capital through funds taken from dormant bank accounts, and loan facilities for social enterprises or charities are offered by several other organisations. The payment-by-results mechanism is yet another kind of social investment – here investors support policy outcomes and, if they are achieved, the government pays a return on capital.

> *Much of the time, religious social innovation was funded as any other charitable activity.*

Tax measures are also important in creating space for social innovation. In the United Kingdom, charities are exempt from some taxes, and since 2014 the government has provided social investment tax relief, offering those investors 30% income tax relief on loans or equity investment into their organisations.[1] The tax relief provides for 'patient capital', since repayments on the principal can't begin until three years after the investment.[2]

how religious social innovation is funded

In theory, what type of funding an organisation – charity, social enterprise, businesses with a social purpose, or Community Interest Company – accesses ought to be determined by the nature of its activity. Innovative social changes may rely on different forms of funding at different stages in their development.

First, as noted above, public money is important in resourcing innovation, and some religious innovation initiatives have managed to bring together private religious philanthropy with public sector support. For example, Safe Families for Children was initially funded by philanthropist Peter Vardy, but a Department for Education Children's Social Care Innovation Fund match-fund has seen the project grow considerably beyond its base in the North East. Effectively, public money directed toward these innovations was a way of leveraging massive volunteer involvement from religious communities – as of March 2016, Safe Families for Children had 2,275 accredited volunteers working across twenty local authorities. Other projects have received some funding at local authority level, while others existed primarily as contract delivery organisations.

There are other notable examples of innovative faith-based projects receiving government funding. Cinnamon Network, a community franchising network, received money from the Cabinet Office Social Action Fund in 2013, and Near Neighbours, a Church Urban Fund-operated community cohesion initiative, has received several rounds of funding amounting to £9.5 million from the Department of Communities and Local Government.

Second, much of the time, religious social innovation was funded as any other charitable activity – through donations and grant making trusts. Local church – based projects were often struggling to find sustainable funding sources, and indeed their needs were often

Faith-based innovations are not accessing all the funding available to others.

'blurry' – for example, where church buildings in which innovative projects were taking place needed repair or development, or where key positions were occupied by clergymen and -women. There was clearly innovation, but it in no way fitted a tidy charitable or social enterprise model, and would be difficult to fund within a social innovation framework.

In the world of religious – particularly Christian – funders, grant-making is therefore a significant driver and supporter of religious social innovation. Nearly all funders support projects which they think will create impact, and want grant recipients to be clear about outputs and outcomes and so on. They have an appetite for innovation, but innovation understood purely as an outcome. Based on our work around Christian funders, a smaller number of funders had shaped their whole grant making approach in order to support religious social innovation. Andrews Charitable Trust, for example, take a 'venture philanthropy' approach, providing funding but also working alongside and developing innovative projects. They fund on the basis of projects being able to identify a priority problem, innovate for impact, provide sustainable solutions, and easily replicate and scale. The Pears Foundation, which established JHub, takes a similar approach, building long term relationships with beneficiaries through cycles of learning and refinement.

how religious social innovation isn't funded

What we see represented in the religious social innovation sector is a healthy mix of funding opportunities, before even taking into account the question of charitable giving from religious individuals (thought to be higher than the national average). Innovation thinking could be more widespread amongst grant-makers, but it is far from absent. Religious organisations have been able to partner with central government for social innovation, on occasion being awarded substantial grants.

There are indications, however, that faith-based innovations are not accessing all the funding available to others in the social innovation space. Thinking about the projects we have offered as case studies in religious social innovation, they were drawing on various 'cocktails' of funding sources, but none had accessed capital markets such as those provided by Big Society Capital.

Ethical cleaning company Clean for Good is an example of a project which is intended to operate commercially as a company limited by shares (see case study below). Tim Thorlby, one of the Directors of Clean for Good and Development Director at the Centre for Theology & Community, articulated the need not to operate as a social enterprise, which could be subsidised with grants. In that case, Clean for Good would not be a demonstration company. Rather, the aspiration was to act as a straight competitor with commercial cleaning companies and therefore show that alternative, socially responsible, business models were viable. It represents an attempt to achieve what the church did not achieve in payday lending.

After a period of development (funded by trusts), investment capital was secured, but this was from a network of partners who were already committed and involved in the cause – Centre for Theology & Community, Church Mission Society, and St Andrew by the Wardrobe – along with individual investors. There are relatively few examples of religious social innovation successfully drawing on sources of social finance, and where there are they – like Clean for Good – seem to be drawing social investment from within the religious world.

It could be that there is a lack of demand – that is, that few religiously-inspired agencies are looking for these kinds of investment. Perhaps they feel, like Clean for Good, that they can best achieve their objectives through charitable grants and individual donations or by sourcing investment 'within the tent'. If so, then the argument would be that there's enough money in the religious world – supplemented by public support for innovation – to support the activity there. There may be an aversion to loan finance, for example, especially when not attached to physical assets.

Alternatively, it may be that there's a supply issue – i.e., that religious social innovation is in need of greater investment, and more diverse kinds of investment, in order to scale and grow in impact, but that there is continued concern about hidden motives or agendas amongst religious organisations, or indeed a feeling that religious social innovation doesn't stand up well against others. Tim Thorlby suggested to us that there were barriers to religion-inspired social causes in the social impact funding world:

> If a church or Christian organisation wants a grant from a secular funder they generally have to pass various additional tests a) that no proselytising is going on, b) that the activity will benefit more than church members, c) sometimes, that the church has a non-church 'community' partner. The working assumption for some seems to be that a church is somehow not a *bona fide* community organisation in itself, and is not representative of the local community and so must be legitimised in some other way.

A third possibility is that there is something about religious social action that makes it inappropriate for capital investment. Certainly, there is a longstanding opinion that – with honourable exceptions – religious institutions are averse to enterprise and markets as drivers for social change. Exploring this goes beyond the scope of this paper, but if correct, it means that a significant seam of religious social innovation remains untapped. Similarly, interviewees suggested to us that there is also resistance to the need to understand and measure impact. Matt Wilson of TLG and social consultancy Goodlabs felt that there were relatively few organisations that were prepared or had capacity to work at the level of sophistication capable of providing the kind of impact measurement that releases social finance:

Interviewees suggested to us that there is also resistance to the need to understand and measure impact.

> A whole new science has emerged on impact and impact measurement… Many faith organisations have a problematic relationship with evidence. They have a view of social change which lends itself to narrative explanations, so the only statistics that the church tend to think about are bums on seats and money in the collection plate.

It's entirely likely that a combination of the factors above collectively mean that religious social innovation isn't funded in the same ways as social innovation in general. Potentially, this could have the effect of inhibiting religious social innovation. If it is to flourish, it may be that it has to self-fund.

institutional investors and religious social innovation

In a notable irony, after Justin Welby's Wonga intervention, an enterprising financial journalist discovered that the Church Commissioners (the body responsible for managing the Church of England's financial reserves and investments) were – via a venture capital fund – investing in Wonga.

Several religious denominations and other religious groups – religious orders, for example – have significant investment portfolios. The Church Investors Group, a collaborative membership organisation for institutional investors, has 59 members who collectively hold around £16 billion in investment assets. Though these holdings are often mocked, as if their mere existence is in contradiction to the church's mission, they usually exist for multiple purposes. The first is to meet ongoing liabilities, such as clergy pensions. The second is to resource the mission of the religious institution in question. In the 2015 annual report, the Church Commissioners report giving away £218.5 million to church based projects, making it one of the largest charitable donors in the United Kingdom (though the largest part of that giving – £122.7 million – went on clergy pension costs).[3]

Currently, religious institutional investors in the United Kingdom are investing responsibly, seeking to exercise their power as shareholders to ensure that investments are consistent with the values of their institution. Increasingly, institutional investors are moving beyond a risk averse 'do no harm' approach into using their influence to encourage change within businesses and markets. They have been active on issues as diverse as climate change, corporate water use and tackling slavery in supply chains.

However, church institutional investors are only starting to look at the scope for creating social value through their investment portfolio. The Church Commissioners, for example, told us that in the last year they had made a $40 million commitment to a US anaerobic digestion fund run by a registered Benefit Company and a £10 million commitment to a UK private equity impact fund whose target areas include renewable energy, vocational education, ethical consumerism and companies addressing the issues of financial exclusion. The challenge to date had been finding investments which "meet… risk/return criteria".

For institutions like the Church Commissioners, there might simply be a change in their grant making approach. They list "contributing to the common good" as a key objective of their approach, and there is no reason why some of their grant funding shouldn't be directed toward religious social innovation, even working with secular social innovation groups to identify, support and scale them. But there is growing interest in instruments like social impact bonds as a new mainstream asset class (and two conferences on impact investing have been held at the Vatican in the last few years). If religious mission is conceived not just as institutional growth but as a broader social impact, then institutional investors have significant potential to help create the funding environment which will support social innovation as a whole, let alone religious social innovation.

Institutional investors have significant potential to help create the funding environment which will support social innovation.

In the next chapter, we turn to consider the place of the final driver of religious social innovation – the presence of religious social innovators.

chapter 2 – references

1   Gov.uk 'Social investment tax relief factsheet'. Available at: https://www.gov.uk/government/
     publications/social-investment-tax-relief-factsheet/social-investment-tax-relief

2   Abigail Rotheroe and Plum Lomax, *Social Investment Tax Relief: Two Years On*, New Philanthropy
     Capital (July 2016) http://www.thinknpc.org/publications/social-investment-tax-relief-sitr/

3   'Investing in the Church's growth', Church Commissioners' Annual Report 2015, https://www.
     churchofengland.org/media/2492846/churchcommissionersar2015.pdf

case study – Clean for Good

Clean for Good is a cleaning company that aims to change the way cleaning services are delivered.

The staff of St Andrew by the Wardrobe in the City of London undertook research into the number and nature of low-paid workers in their parish and found a surprising number – including many cleaners. The church began to ask how they could help them. The sector is one which is notorious for low pay, poor conditions, a lack of good people management, and unpredictability of working hours and income. The Church began to explore the possibility of launching an ethical cleaning company.

Miriam Goodacre, a staff member at the church at the time, pitched the idea to a dragon's den-style forum run by the Church Mission Society and won the competition. CMS invited her to a week-long 'intensive' supporting missional entrepreneurs, to help develop the idea. It began to gather momentum and support, which eventually saw the Centre for Theology & Community, the Church Mission Society, and St Andrew by the Wardrobe collaborate to create a company limited by shares: Clean for Good.

The aim is to create a 'good' cleaning company which would deliver a good professional service and also pay the Living Wage to all of its staff, manage them well and invest in their development. They intend to compete on a level playing field with other cleaning companies in the sector, not as a subsidised social enterprise, and thus become a demonstration company – one that 'disrupts' and provokes change in the sector.

The insight at the heart of the business is a lack of transparency in the supply chain. Services are contracted out on the basis of cost rather than on the treatment of workers, but because the workers are 'hidden' (often outsourced), few companies are aware of the implications of their procurement decisions. Although it aims to be a profitable business on issues like wage rates, Clean for Good's core purpose, which would be maintained by the shareholders, is to change the way that cleaning is done in London. It describes itself as 'a business with a social purpose'.

Tim Thorlby, Development Director at the Centre for Theology & Community and one of the directors of Clean for Good, agrees that the company faces significant hurdles – not least the fact that procurement decisions are often made with a view to keeping costs down – but says that treating people better means paying them more. The business' future success therefore relies on persuading companies of the moral, ethical, social, and business case for paying more for their cleaners – persuading them that "every cleaner has a story".

what's the social innovation?

Clean for Good is an ambitious social transformation project, with a key insight on the 'real problem' – low wages, poor conditions and poor management are symptoms of a procurement which preferences price above all else, and where cleaners are 'invisible'. The business model is a novel way (for a church and church charities) of achieving the social goal, which is about system transformation rather than symptom amelioration. It also demonstrates the need for innovation infrastructure – institutions that can help the helpers, in this instance provided by Church Mission Society and the Centre for Theology & Community. In spite of the significant potential social impact, Clean for Good has had to raise its own funds and source pro bono legal support to establish the business.

driver: social entrepreneurs

In the preceding chapters we have argued for a broad approach to social innovation, one that sees it as a process undergirded by attitudes, rather than fixating on the outcome. We have also highlighted the need to focus on the networks, communities and collaboration that encourage and support innovation – the engine of innovation; and on more diverse forms of funding – the fuel of innovation – rather than on the individual entrepreneur. In this final chapter, however, we turn to consider the question of leadership and the place of the religious social innovator or entrepreneur.

the myth of the heroic innovator

Daniela Papi-Thornton, deputy director of the Skoll Centre for Social Entrepreneurship, writes in the *Stanford Social Innovation Review*, that:

> We have entered the era of *heropreneurship*, where reverence for the heroic social entrepreneur has led countless people to pursue a career path that promises opportunities to save the world, gain social status, and earn money, all at the same time.

She observes how many social entrepreneurs in waiting wanted to solve problems that they have never experienced, such as "building an app for African farmers when the founding team has neither farmed nor been to Africa". They had all the knowledge and training to start a social business, but none of the skills it takes to really understand a problem.[1]

The image of a bespectacled Silicon Valley alumnus throwing technology at entrenched social problems in the full confidence that he can succeed where hundreds before have failed is one of the images that give the idea of social innovation a bad name – charity, but with just an extra helping of cool, or is it arrogance? It is Schumpeter's 'heroic entrepreneur' reincarnated.

> *Culture determines how easy life will be even for the most spirited innovators.*

There are real problems with this vision of innovation, particularly when it assumes that social goods and profit can easily be pursued together in all contexts. There is a link between individual entrepreneurial spirit and an appetite for innovation, but it is one factor among many others. In particular, culture determines how easy life will be even for the most spirited innovators. Commentators have noted that Japan is a difficult context in which to be an innovator: "the social costs of pursuing risk – and potentially failing – are still very high".[2]

Happily, social innovators actually don't tend to look like this stereotype. Papi-Thornton points to "a more holistic set of skills", including problem definition, the ability to make disjointed systems work together, and being able to realistically assess their role in solving problems. In religious language, a social innovator is more likely to be wise, loving, and humble than she is to conform to the image of a *heropreneur*. That said, social innovators may not find it easy to negotiate the institutional religious landscape.

meet the religious social innovators

On the basis of interviews conducted with religious social innovators and those working with social innovators, it's possible to identify key skills or characteristics. It's important to know these things, because making space for them will be a vital component of creating greater space for innovation.

problem definers

Tim Curtis, a lecturer in social and community development at Northampton University and author on social innovation, identifies problem definition as a key priority for social innovators.

> There's a tendency in religious and secular organisations to say, "This is what we know, and we're going to go and tackle the problems that we know, as opposed to knowing what the real problems are". There's a lack of skill around the problem analysis and problem framing. You have to ask how you conceptualise the problem before you design an appropriate response.

Curtis argues that the community connectedness of religious organisations could, on the one hand, be an advantage for religious organisations in knowing how to conceptualise problems, but on the other it could, paradoxically, also be a way that religious communities set themselves apart from others. Classically, most religious networks have 'bonding social capital' – fewer have 'bridging capital'. Problem definition relies on being close enough to communities to have proper insight into the problems they face. As one interviewee put it, "We spend too much time going to the wrong place and asking the wrong people the wrong question at the wrong time – no surprises we come up with the wrong feckin' answer."

The social innovators we spoke to made similar points. Sally Smith from Sanctus St Mark's conceptualised 'the problem' as no problem at all. In spite of their material and practical needs, the presence of asylum seekers and refugees in Stoke-on-Trent was not only a difficulty to be negotiated but rather a gift to be appropriately received. They could bring richness and, in some cases, considerable skill and resilience to a struggling city like Stoke-on-Trent.

Tim Thorlby from Clean for Good described some of the listening actions they had undertaken with cleaners, identifying problems that few had pinpointed before. Cost-cutting had led to a stripping back of middle management in cleaning agencies, meaning that cleaners working on contracts for high street names were almost completely unmanaged. "One lady told me that she had met her manager twice – once on her first day in the role, and then again three months later when he came to tell her that he had resigned". This led them to identify consistent management as a key priority of the business – less eye catching than guaranteeing a set number of hours or living wage rates of pay, but vital to the wellbeing of cleaners.

This was one of the problems facing religious social innovators. It could be hard to persuade people with a fixed idea of 'what the problem is' that they might be missing something important. A Christian lawyer and trustee of the Real Junk Food project said that churches "got the food poverty angle, and want to help. What they don't get is that there's a massive problem to do with the food supply system, which sees a third effectively go to landfill". Ian Soars, Director of Fegans, said that religious organisations, in spite of their social justice aspirations, could be fearful of the sheer need they would uncover if they began to think of problems in systematic ways. Amongst established organisations, there could also be an unwillingness to let go of treasured approaches, even though the context may have changed radically.

> *It can be hard to persuade people with a fixed idea of 'what the problem is' that they might be missing something important.*

collaborators

After Welby's Wonga intervention, a group of social innovators did start working on a social Wonga. Rev Philip Krinks – a Church of England vicar and Director of the St Martin's Partnership – thought that a responsible lender, who would struggle to compete because of the high costs and risks of working with less wealthy customers, could operate by reducing the costs and operating online. Krinks developed an outline business case and approached social investors with the proposal. They advised him to work with Street UK, a secular social enterprise, who were already providing affordable finance in the West Midlands. As a Community Interest Company, Street UK could accept social finance to fund a loan book, where credit unions could not. Street UK launched its online lending platform – Track Loans – in May 2016.[3]

The story is emblematic of a willingness to work across the boundaries of sacred and secular with a view to achieving a social goal. Krinks was clear that, even when such innovations had been effectively realised, they were only part of the solution.

> To me this is an example of an area where you need more than one horse in the race. It takes a variety of different institutions working together to create good outcomes – a just system. You need credit unions, you need these financial social enterprises, responsible finance providers, you need debt counselling charities. The risk in a conversation like this is once you've decided which horse you're going to back you criticise all the other horses. But actually they're all needed. Street UK can't hold anyone's deposit, so we're not answering that question.

The image of the individual entrepreneur is a powerful one, but it is in no way representative of religious social innovators.

The image of the individual entrepreneur is a powerful one, but it is in no way representative of religious social innovators. They took the view that social change was hard work, and their innovations – true to the definition – were social by means as well as by objective.

Clearly, not all partnerships with all agencies were fruitful. One interviewee observed that their working relationship with their local authority around one innovation should not be described as a 'partnership' at all. Budget cuts had meant that many of the strategic thinkers in the authority had gone and that their staff were wholly absorbed in simply meeting regulatory and legislative minimums. Equally, some interviewees were frustrated by a lack of willingness amongst religious institutional gatekeepers to collaborate in religious social innovation.

leadership

A key problem for religious social innovators is that they are often perceived within religious organisations to be engaged in a secondary level of mission, separate from the institution's core mission. This of course would apply to any form of social action – but perhaps particularly in cases where social innovators wanted to challenge established norms about what counted as 'doing good'. Matt Wilson of Goodlabs said:

> Perhaps this goes all the way back to Acts 6 and the division of social ministries from ministry of the Word… It's certainly a shame that none of the twelve opted to lead in the sphere of social ministry. I would say this has undoubtedly led to a hierarchy, with the Word ministry on top and social ministry beneath. As a national leader in social ministries for 20 years I feel this very keenly and would go so far as to say it is endemic.

There was a sense that this might set them at something of cross purposes with the organisation. Many innovators were 'intrapreneurs' as well as entrepreneurs, trying to reform their own institution or urge it to use its resources for social purposes. Religious social innovation often seems to be about scaling social responses through drawing on the volunteering power of the local church – many innovators stood with one foot outside church or religious networks, finding ways to convince and appeal to religious leaders and to recognise their cause and support and participate in it. Predictably, they were sometimes successful, and sometimes not. The most commonly cited clash was between different visions of religious mission – the spiritual before social versus the social before spiritual. Ian Soars from Fegans said:

> I've spent a lot of time with vicars and ministers from Catholic [and] Protestant churches, Anglicans, Baptists. I've spent a lot of time with these guys. There does seem to be just two straightforward groups – people who get it, and people who don't. People that have a heart for the community and people that haven't… Those that do get it are passionately proud of what they believe in, but they know that they're there to love their neighbour.

Ultimately, those with an instinct and aptitude for social innovation will likely find some mechanism through which to address the needs which they see in society. Whether they act through and with religious institutions depends, in large part, on the breadth of the institution's understanding of mission. If religious networks genuinely value social transformation, then they must look for ways to support and resource religious social innovators.

space for religious innovators

The social sector has been persuaded of the need for social innovation. Larger charities have innovation departments, and even smaller ones have dedicated members of staff who have the task of embedding innovation into the organisation, and the wider social innovation community is blessed with a network of hubs, incubators, labs and accelerator programmes which provide coaching and guidance for social innovators, again pointing to a greater sense of intentionality around social change.

There is a need to legitimate social entrepreneurship as a significant vocation – as important as more traditionally 'religious' forms of ministry.

We have already argued that there is relatively little innovation 'infrastructure', which can leave individuals short of the training, resources or guidance they might need. In what other ways could the religious world make the life of the social innovator a more comfortable one?

First, there is a need to legitimate social entrepreneurship as a significant vocation – as important as more traditionally 'religious' forms of ministry. Religious networks rightly focus on identifying, recruiting and deploying future leaders, but in their training and development they don't focus on public or social action. This is not to say that every priest should be a social worker, but that lay leaders should be supported and encouraged as they try and learn their craft.

Second, there should be the recognition that social innovation is a corporate endeavour – or "social in means and ends". Religious institutions often have significant power to bring people together around common goals. They could do more to bring together their own activists with others from whom they can learn.

chapter 3 – references

1   Daniela Papi-Thornton, 'Tackling Heropreneurship', *Stanford Social Innovation Review*, 23 February 2016 https://ssir.org/articles/entry/tackling_heropreneurship

2   Kondo, 'Old problems, new solutions' (op, cit.) p. 30.

3   https://www.trackloans.co.uk

case study – Sanctus St Mark's

When Rev Sally Smith became the Vicar of St Mark's Shelton in Stoke-on-Trent in 2013, one of its existing activities was a craft group for refugee women. After a while, men began to turn up too. The craft group eventually closed but the doors remained open, and a growing number of people would attend drop in sessions. Initially, reported Smith, it was a matter of opening the door and putting the kettle on.

Stoke-on-Trent is a Home Office dispersal area, and the drop-in sessions in churches in Shelton and Longton quickly grew. They are now attended by hundreds of people per week with a variety of needs.

Sanctus St Mark's formally incorporated as a Community Interest Company in 2014. Practically, the project provides a foodbank, clothing, toiletries and household goods, English language and literacy support, and informal advice – and emotional support – during the asylum application process. They have also persuaded church members to buy houses in the area, which are used to accommodate asylum seekers who have no recourse to public funds.

The drop-ins also act as 'hubs' where asylum seekers can access support from other parties, such as a dedicated asylum and refugee health support team from Stoke on Trent PCT, or advice from the Citizens' Advice Bureau.

Smith experienced opposition from members of her church, who didn't think that the church should be so focused on helping refugees and asylum seekers. Many left. The life of the church, including its Sunday services, is now marked by the presence of a diverse, multi-racial and multi-ethnic community.

what's the social innovation?

What sets Sanctus St Mark's apart from the many other projects that provide support for asylum seekers and refugees? It's an impressive project, but is it social innovation?

First, Sally Smith is a religious 'intrapreneur' who has taken the limited resources available to a dwindling congregation, and refocused them on an outward mission, sadly to the frustration of some of her early congregants. Second, the project incorporates aspects of enterprise, not least in persuading people to invest significant amounts of money in housing in the local area. Third, there's an insight – namely that 'the problem' isn't just one of material lack, but of isolation. Sanctus St Mark's *provides* various important services – but it *is* a community.

conclusion

How could faith-based organisations do good, better?

As things stand, the engine, fuel, and drivers of religious social action are aligned perfectly to produce exactly what we see in terms of religious social action. Nearly all of which is highly commendable – but, as one interviewee put it, "we do good, but not good enough". The most pessimistic view is that institutions, finance and leadership interact in such a way as to deliver services that may or may not resolve the problems we intend to tackle, at a limited scale, without accessing emerging forms of social finance, and where social entrepreneurs and innovators will be perceived as acting outside the core mission of religious networks.

More positively, there are organisations and individuals who are thinking and acting innovatively. They show a level of ambition and trust in human creativity and agency, and have an intentional and reflective approach to social change. They look to embed innovation as a process – a new approach to social change.

In this report we have explored different aspects of religious social innovation.

In the first chapter we looked at the institutional context – what we have called the engine of social innovation. We argued that while there are cultural and linguistic barriers between social innovation and religion, these can be overcome by building on a significant history of social innovation and by building a theological case in different ways in different traditions. A more significant barrier to religious social innovation is the lack of the kind of institutional framework which creates space for innovation. Religious institutions can also be poor at embedding processes which allow for innovation – religious social innovation therefore tends to progress not within religious institutions, but alongside and outside of them.

In the second chapter we looked at the question of the fuel for religious social innovation. While there are many potential sources, from charitable trusts through to statutory funding and venture philanthropy, we argued that – while there has been some progress – religious social action has not yet been able to fully tap some of the new social funding that has come on stream. We suggested that barriers might include a continued suspicion of faith-based actors, but also an aversion to more sophisticated approaches to impact measurement.

The third chapter looked at the drivers – that is, social leaders, innovators and entrepreneurs. Key traits include problem definition, collaboration, and an appetite for risk. We argued, however, that they can be marginalised in religious networks.

How, then, to create a context where faith-based organisations can do good better?

Tuning the engine

1.   The first recommendation is predictable, but faith-based organisations should give greater attention to innovation. This is essential in the present environment, where more is expected from civil society organisations than ever. For many, this will not look like presenting some staggering new insight or programme, but simply continuing to peel back the layers of the problem and ask how they can have a greater impact than ever. Religious organisations should be about doing more, but also doing better. There is a place for more theoretical and theological work around social innovation.

2.   Religious charities could start small when it comes to innovation. Focusing on the output model of innovation misses the importance of embedding the culture and processes of innovation. Larger religious charities should be asking how they can focus resources on innovation – perhaps by identifying members of staff who should focus on innovation – but even relatively small charities could and should be asking how they can generate greater impact, whether that is through accessing tools which will help them monitor impact or learning from and working with others.

3.   Religious groups should closely monitor innovations which seek to use markets and enterprise as ways to achieve social change. This is far from an easy option, but such interventions have the potential to move beyond poverty alleviation and amelioration into transformative social engagement.

4.   There is a case for new organisations and institutions which explicitly focus on religious social innovation in different communities, similar to JHub – the Jewish social innovation hub. Far from being simply a fashionable bandwagon, such an organisation would exist to provide practical support to the real challenges faced by religious social innovators, such as developing the metrics that will unlock funding.

These would provide support for social innovators, turning ideas into genuinely scalable models of social change and transformation.

Using the best fuel

1.   There is considerable appetite amongst faith-funders for innovative solutions, but funders need to be careful to pursue it intelligently. Religious charitable trusts could create dedicated innovation funds which look to invest in both innovative projects and processes for existing organisations to push their work on to another stage.

2.   Faith-based charities need to be better at identifying priorities and tracking impact – this will create access to forms of finance and opportunities for scale that hitherto have not been available to religious organisations. The best examples of innovation we have explored know what they want to do and how well they are doing it. They are willing to be held accountable against social outcomes. Innovation can still undergird holistic and relational interventions, but those interventions will still need to be articulated and evidenced.

3.   There needs to be systematic engagement with social innovation funders in order to understand what, if anything, prevents them from engaging more with religious groups. Fears around the 'problem of proselytism' have been allayed for many statutory funders through greater transparency and assurances – the same can be done for corporates and social funders.

4.   There is a significant space which has yet to be properly explored – that is of the potential for social value in the portfolio of religious institutional investors. Distributing the proceeds of socially responsible investment is a positive model, but the missional potential of investing for social value is enormous. At the least, institutional investors should consider small trials.

Finding the best drivers

1.   At present, too many religious social entrepreneurs end up taking their skills and abilities out of the tent. Social action has been seen as a bolt-on to religious networks – social entrepreneurs and innovators can seem disruptive, asking questions around how resources are directed within a religious denomination. Religious groups need to support social innovators within their ranks by recognising and developing their skills, and acknowledging social change as an important vocation in its own right, rather than a clerical hobby.

2.   Religious organisations often have significant convening power. They could support religious social innovators by drawing them together with others, promoting collaboration between different individuals and organisations on given social goals.

There are barriers and dissonances between religion and innovation. Religious traditions are exactly that – traditions. It is not that they are not open to change, but they are rooted in ways of thinking and of doing (and also of not-doing) that are open to evolution, but not revolution. As theologian Jaroslav Pelikan said, capturing the tension nicely, "Tradition is the living faith of the dead, traditionalism is the dead faith of the living."[1] Another theologian, L Gregory Jones, has called for 'traditioned' innovation:

> Traditioned innovation honors and engages the past while adapting to the future because it forces us to ask fundamental questions about who we are and what purpose we have for existing: Who have we been, and now, in shifting circumstances, who will we continue to be? How will we stay true to the End, to which God calls us, while adapting to new circumstances? How do we ensure our "why" doesn't change even as we innovate and adapt to changing circumstances?[2]

The appropriate analogy for a religious social innovator would not be the CEO of a tech start-up, but a craftsman or woman who having inhabited a long heritage of practice continues to practice it in a different environment meeting contemporary needs and aspirations. Our social, economic and political context is changing rapidly and will continue to do so. Faithfully pursuing the common good is unlikely to look like doing the same thing over and over again.

conclusion – references

1   Jaroslav Pelikan, *The Vindication of Tradition: The 1983 Jefferson Lecture in the Humanities* (Yale University Press, 1986), p. 65.

2   Jones, L. Gregory, *Christian Social Innovation: Renewing Wesleyan Witness* (Abingdon Press, 2016) Kindle Locations 717-720.